In Search of Equilibrium

In Search of Equilibrium

Theresa Lola

Nine
Arches
Press

In Search of Equilibrium
Theresa Lola

ISBN: 9781911027683

Cover artwork: 'In the lonely hour (I)' © Obi Chigozie.
www.facebook.com/theartofobichigozie
www.Instagram.com/gozie.o

First published February 2019 by:

Nine Arches Press
Unit 14, Sir Frank Whittle Business Centre,
Great Central Way, Rugby.
CV21 3XH
United Kingdom

www.ninearchespress.com

Printed in the United Kingdom by:
Imprint Digital

Nine Arches Press is supported using public funding
by Arts Council England.

Supported using public funding by
ARTS COUNCIL
ENGLAND

*For my grandfather, for family, for faith,
and the memories that shake them.*

Contents

The Unedited Version of The Lord's Prayer 9

Equilibrium 10

Alzheimer's Algorithm 11

Sing with Me and Do Not Die of Thirst 14

wikiHow To Find Things You Have Lost 16

Death: Definitions (I) 18

Friday the 13th 19

Insomnia is a Cheap Drug 20

Lean Back as Instructed by Fat Joe 21

Crisis 22

ode to edge control gel 24

Sight Test 25

The Pastor's Daughter Refuses to be a Circle 26

Black Marilyn 27

wikiHow To Mourn: Mourning in Healthy Ways 28

Removed from the Edge 30

Balloons 31

Judas 32

Closer 33

A Shattered Ghazal On Understanding Existence 37

Dead Man Walking 38

Tailoring Grief 39

Reporting Live from Grandpa's Funeral 40

The Vow 42

Pass the Parcel 43

<h>Cutting Back on Work Shifts </h1> 44

Moving on is Involuntary 45

Death: Definitions (II) 46

Lazarus 47

Blessed Are the Mothers of a Dead Child 48

We Rebuke This Bad Death 49

Swimming   50
Staying Alive   51
Where is Ja Rule to Make Sense of the Apocalypse   52
Death Definition (III)   54
Portrait of Jesus in a Blue Robe   55
Psalm 151   56

Notes   58
Thanks and Acknowledgements   59

The Unedited Version of The Lord's Prayer

[1] Our Father, who art in heaven,
shadow be thy face
[2] for thy kingdom has been obstructed
by my grandfather forgetting my name.
Thy will be done
in his body, maybe
[3] God's will is a butcher's knife that cuts into one flesh
to feed another a plate of life lessons.
[4] I swallowed my grandfather's suffering
and my belly is bloated with life lessons.
I guess thy will be done in his body,
But on the condition he ends up in heaven.
[5] A man can't ask for forgiveness for sins he can't remember.

[6] Give us a day
where my grandfather's hands break bread
during dinner as he talks to us about Nigerian politics.
[7] Give us a day
where my grandfather's bladder
is not a torn cloud vomiting a flood.
[8] Give me a day
where my grandfather is telling me about the healing
powers of the Aloe Vera plants in his garden.

[9] My grandmother scrubs the urine off his body.
[10] This is love, this is not a trespassing,
she need not ask for forgiveness.
[11] Lead us not into temptation
to curse thy name.
[12] My grandmother holds the rosary beads
like a line of pills she wants to overdose on.

[13] Faith is all I know, is the cloth I shield my grief in,
even when I fear God might be a thin shadow.

Equilibrium

My new-born brother wailed into existence
and my grandfather's eyes became two stopwatches

counting down his own exit. At the naming ceremony
my grandfather was quiet as a body cut open for autopsy.

He broke bread, sipped on fresh orange juice.
The pause between each sip elongated and I knew

the mathematician in him
had remembered the equation of equilibrium.

As my new-born brother was crowned with a name
my grandfather's brain began to forget his.

Alzheimer's Algorithm

IF

the protein 'tau' that assists transfer of information
between brain cells becomes a virus.

OUTPUT
Your grandfather's memory folder erases.

His children crawl back into his wife's womb.

The grandchildren fade

into a web of distant concepts.

He tries to access his wedding pictures,

but they keep saving as pixelated images.

He tries to outsmart Alzheimer's

by storing his wife's scent in an encrypted folder

so it is never stolen from his memory.

The family tries to pull through

and prevent the dinner table from looking

like a photograph with the faces cropped out.

Your grandfather desperately tries to restart

his memory, but his skull is a dented button.

IF

the bridge between the brain
and the bowel/bladder breaks down

OUTPUT

the bandwidth of your grandfather's brain is too low

to receive warnings fast enough

when urine is leaking from his bladder.

Your grandmother becomes the lifeguard

dragging his body to the toilet

to stop him from drowning.

IF

(a == the affected realises they are losing control of their body

or

 b== after a long search your grandfather is returned home
after being found wandering the streets with his laptop
claiming he is on his way to work)

OUTPUT:

Your grandfather, a computer engineer,

can't find a way to exit/   /the screen

when he realises he is in the final level of Alzheimer's.

His thin body swings/   /between

moods like an umbrella drunk on the wind.

He communicates his sadness and lack of appetite

by crashing/   /the plate

of pounded yam and eforiro to the floor.

He walks into a room and your breath weighs/   /heavier

than a stack of unfinished letters.

You cope with the trauma of seeing him like this

by cutting/   /and pasting

the old version of himself over his body.

Sing with Me and Do Not Die of Thirst

Alzheimer's patients sing every lyric to their favourite songs,
and this casual act becomes a dance with defiance.
Research shows our memory of music remains intact,
like the clothes of a missing child kept by a mother;
the brain stores music in a different place,
—a subtle precaution.

My grandmother bathes my grandfather
and lyrics spill from his mouth
like water from a drowned child.
He sings Johnny Nash's 'I Can See Clearly Now'
in a bass so sharp it cuts the water in half
to form a space my grandmother can walk through.
He saw water: his brain's automatic response was
to regurgitate a song that had the word 'rain' in it.
My grandmother takes in his voice
and her skin splits open like an overstuffed suitcase.
My God, it must hurt for someone you love
to remember a song in clearer detail than your face.

She wonders how he knows to accentuate *blue ska-yeee-aies*.
Proof that music muscle memory
can stretch more than shaki meat.
My grandmother joins in to harmonise,
the Bible says two shall become one voice and live till
death cracks the voice in half; I paraphrased out of anger.
Her voice is shaky as waist beads on a Fela Kuti back-up dancer,
grief tugs on your vocal chords like heavy braids,
leaves it with sore and thinning edges.

As they harmonise my grandmother morphs into the song,
wipes water from her husband's face, sings
I can see clearly now the rain is gone,
and once again they are two vivacious youths
whirling though a garden in summer.

He says, "you look like the girl Mona I danced with"
and the water in the bathtub levitates to become rain.

wikiHow To Find Things You Have Lost

(1) Try to remember the last time you had the item.

The last time I saw my grandfather with his memory was two months ago,
it danced on his tongue as he taught me about gardening,
about how you can never predict which plant will be weakened by weeds.

(2) Think of everywhere you went since you lost the item.

My grandfather spends most days ransacking hell;
hell is the heat of our crowded breaths asking why
he no longer remembers us.

There are two things to do when looking for the item:

(a) Try to get in the mindset you had when you lost the item.

My grandfather was a patient man,
but patience is useless to a man being pinned to a target by a clock.
Each family member waters the parched mouth of their search
with a can of anger in hope it will hasten the growth of answers.

(b) Be positive and relaxed when searching for your item.

When my grandfather transforms into Edward Scissorhands
we force pills down his throat to detach the blades.

(3) Retrace your steps.

I asked my grandfather when he first noticed loss of memory, he said
it could be that time   *I was catching up with a friend*
and the wind was a vulture snatching words   from my mouth.
It could be that time
I was ironing my tie for work   and Mona reminded me I had retired
from the computer firm years earlier.   It could be that time
I hid in my room for days after the mirror called me   an intruder

It could be that time   I went for a walk
        and my legs felt like two faulty compasses
until the dark green painted mama-put shop told me I was
never far away from   home.

(4) Search thoroughly for your item.

I led my grandfather to the tomato stew pot in the kitchen
and prayed for him to inhale memories.
Grandma says the aroma of food is a nest
where vivid memories of when it mingled with us is stored.
The smoke from the stew thick with Maggi cubes rose up
to his nose like a sky lantern released by a grieving loved one,
and my grandfather became a trigger spilling with memories.
He told us stories of Sundays when his children and we
the grandchildren gathered to feast on jollof rice and plantain.
To keep the triggers pouring I begged him to search my face;
though I do not resemble him, I can recite back our conversations
in his spitting image.

(5) Ask for help.

We have prayed to God for his healing to arrive quicker, made it clear
we don't want to be lab rats used to test the stretch of faith.
We asked the doctor for help and the doctor claimed this loss
can never be recovered, and neither can the body.
Call me pessimistic, but what difference does it make anyway,
man can only delay death, not stop it.

(6) Take a break.

My grandfather has stopped searching for his memory,
I tried resuming the search,
but he refused, he does not remember what he is looking for.

Death: Definitions (I)

/dɛθ/

noun

The plague that whittled down my family size
by one less grandfather.

Or

The tool that maintains equilibrium;
one human exits earth for one new one to enter.

Friday the 13th

Every year my grandfather is not alive
my grandmother blows out candles on a cake
spongy as a corpse and celebrates the parts of him
living in her grandchildren.

I am sure someone will miss me
when my age becomes a stagnant number.
If not, I'll wave from heaven,
even if the world dismisses it as a violent wind.

My mother danced into my room with a candle-lit
birthday cake, the fire rose to form a chandelier.
She poured a song into my small hands
like medicine poured into a teaspoon.

Later, I went into school with my birthday badge
to remind the class I am not dead. Emma murmured
"no one cares". She was a generous beast,
she gave her teeth to everyone I met later in life.

Insomnia is a Cheap Drug

Cause of use	Anyone who is hungry for a way to elongate the erasure of themselves will experiment with methods. Sadness is the silent syllable in every stored sound you know, your brain is in desperate need of emptying its memories, and not everyone wants to wait till their 60s for the body to naturally begin to forget or for a prayer to return with results.
How it was first discovered	After multiple sleepless nights your tired brain only stored blurred versions of the images of you demolishing your body into a sea of sand. You were intrigued by how lack of sleep impairs the brain's ability to learn and retain information, so you began to use this as a method of forgetting yourself.
Effect of use	The morning after a sleepless night feels like hallucination. You do not need a drug when all you have to do is pop your eyes open like pills for a few nights, and your brain will start to stagger like a drunk with fractured recollections. No new word carved in the shape of a weapon can rest in your mind long enough. The Hippocampus shrinks and your most vivid memory from breakfast is fire kissing the scalp of a pot. Slowly, the neocortex sheds long-term memories; you have no vivid images of days you hated yourself, days your umbilical cord grew back and tried to strangle you.
Side Effects	There is no downside to the side effects. When people ask why you are irritable as a balloon rubbing against fire or when they ask why you are as quick to use your fist as ears, all you say is that you haven't slept in days.

Lean Back as instructed by Fat Joe

in one of the greatest Hip Hop songs of all time. You stand in front of a mirror, lean your right shoulder backwards at a 45-degree angle; by the time you return to the mirror your bones have stretched into hangers draped with gold chains.

You wear arrogance like a rented wedding dress. You accessorise it with the lyrics you memorise during lunch breaks, with no one to tell you to quiet the noise. This is new to you, a joy that makes you feel like you are moonwalking on God's eyelashes.

Hip Hop is the unofficial national anthem at school. When the students gather you recite the lyrics to Lean Back, lean your shoulder at a 45-degree angle and watch them gaze at the perfect arch, your tongue burning with no lyric left un-scraped.

Till now you carried the name 'unidentified female body in yearbook pictures'. You tried scratching out the name, shifted to the busy table at the cafeteria; but forget subtlety – sometimes you need a kind of confidence you can dangle on your neck like a shark on a hook. An act of pretence, to tell others you wear shinier ghosts, shimmy your name in their face. What better instructor to mimic if not Hip Hop?

You watch as your name gets pinned to a notice board of tongues. Their tongues touch your name like hands reaching for the garment of Jesus. You pose for the new yearbook picture, chains dangling on your weak neck.

This was never you, but who wouldn't stretch their body into a flag to avoid being deported back into their shadow?

Crisis

Does your mother know you are here?
No, but she knows I left,
my skin is draped over her Bible
waiting for the day I return back to my body. Maybe

I am flirting with death
because I am still star-struck from seeing a corpse
for the first time. My grandfather's body

lay in his casket no longer troubled
by the organs that played sad music
in his body.

I am here because I am looking for other ways
to solve my crisis aside from selling my body
to the bottom of an ocean.

Are you afraid of suicide?
I am afraid of hell,
I am afraid the ocean
is just a bedsheet covering a layer of fire underneath.

I am here because ten years have passed
and the voices of bullies are still jammed in my ear,
surgeons will not remove what they cannot see.

Childhood trauma affects
mental and physical health in adulthood.
The past hangs over me
like clothes on a washing line.
Look at me.

Look at me, I am a droplet of knives.
Look at me, I am a jellyfish stinging itself.
Look at me, shame is the only asset I have in stock.

Are you happy for us to continue with the sessions?
Yes please, happy I found a black woman, but right now
I have student loan to repay, and I owe God. My last
cheque bounced off a cloud and fell like a hailstone.

ode to edge control gel

You body of viscous liquid that drapes my hair into a cape to conceal my shame. You italicise my insecurity so it reads like sleeked-back baby hairs. I had become the people I chuckled at, I would tweet #noedges and pour my laughter in between the thin hair strands of others. You loosened Karma's buckle on me, reduced the number of eyes gawking at the naked circle of scalp on my edges. It was not the domineering tug of weaves or braids that caused my breakage. The void inside me had replicated itself on my scalp, spread its fire to my hair strands and turned my edges into an extinct forest. My mother and I listened as the doctor said hair loss can be the body's reaction to stress, asked if it was due to my exams, or boy trouble; I had no answer. Sometimes it's impossible to tie your hollowness to tangible things. Doctor handed me a white cream to rub out the indignity, told me to give the wait for hair growth a few weeks. While I waited you leapt in without asking for a backstory. You poured shine to my thin hair edges as if to say my crown deserves to be polished, even when a jewel is missing.

Sight Test

During dinner with my mother I am trying
not to blink too much or the word *therapy*
might slip from the folds of my eyelids
like a pole from a scaffolded building,
turn my mother into a dented door frame.
The eyes cannot keep a secret,
they blab about what the body is going through,
play dead to signal a carcass inside your ribcage.
The therapist is training my eyes
to swallow more light
so I can view
the alleyway
in my lungs when disposing of depression.
Back from work, my mother
is detailing what she saw in a patient's eyes,
speaks of the girl who would have gone blind
if her retinal detachment were not spotted so quickly.
I chew my tongue into gasps in response to her stories.
I made her dinner to relieve her stress. We are lounging
in a bright living room. When you are running from the dark
even a light bulb will feel like God's eye socket.
I can tell my mother I went to a therapy session,
there will be no harm, but the words are stuck in my eyelids.
I will tell her once the miracle has come to pass.
She asks if she can test her new optical instrument on me,
I reply *which eye should we start with?*

The Pastor's Daughter Refuses to be a Circle

You are a diameter slicing your mother in half
      and crucifying Jesus in the centre.
A circumference of prayers has yet to circle you back to God.
      You defend yourself as good enough,
a rebel to the strict rules for holiness.
      The aunties wearing hats as big as their mouths
shake their heads like a tambourine
      when they see your seat empty in church.

Your mother etches scriptures on your tongue,
      says you are destined to become a prophet
because you once had a dream about hell.
      You just want to be a child,
fantasise about an earth
      where the explanation for grey clouds is simply rain.

When your mother circles the house spewing out prayers,
      you walk past her so fast your body splits open the air.
If you make a mother choose between God and her child
      she will slice her body in half to be available for both.

Your mother shapes her mouth into an aggressive circle
      and urges you to get ready for church.
You wear the same outfit every Sunday: a stubborn spirit.
      The sermon today was on hell.
After church, you lay in bed and curve your body into itself.
      You are a moon being pierced by its own edges.

Black Marilyn

In Lagos, a photograph of Marilyn Monroe watches me
in my hotel room as I scrub my body
like it's a house preparing for an estate agent's visit.
I think Marilyn wants to say something to me,
the way her mouth is always open
like a cheating husband's zipper.

My mind carries more weapons
than all war-torn countries combined.
Every day I survive is worth a medal or two.
I celebrate by buying more clothes than I can afford.
I must be rich; my void is always building
a bigger room to accommodate new things.

Today I woke up surprised I was still alive,
last thing I remember was my body swinging
from a ceiling of inadequacies.
In my head I have died in so many ways
I must be a god the way I keep resurrecting
into prettier caskets.

Marilyn's photographer, Lawrence Schiller, said
Marilyn was afraid that she was nothing more
than her beauty.
You can call me arrogant, call me black Marilyn,
come celebrate with me,
I am so beautiful death can't take its eyes off me.

wikiHow To Mourn: Mourning in Healthy Ways

(1) Acknowledge your emotions in order to begin the healing process.

I am a planet orbiting a black hole/burial site/border/broken-heart
in search of a creation story where I remain alive/awake/angelic
when he leaves.

(2) Express your feelings through a tangible medium.

Take this poem as an elegy of one-sided truths
about an ended relationship.
The body is the best conductor of grief.

(3) Acknowledge that your grief is yours.

Grief is the most expensive thing I own. I hide it in a safe box,
I admit I only wear it for special occasions where men will bid
        to buy it off me.

(4) Maintain your physical health.

Before I painted my nails bright orange to make the sun jealous,
I was grey as a skinless moon, didn't shower for days,
even the walls of my room leaned in to check up on me.
My hair ate itself for lunch, left me with a bald plate for edges.
The body is feeble; negotiate with it on ways to feel beautiful again.

(5) Avoid using alcohol, drugs, or food to deal with your grief.

When he left I dived into glasses of wine like each one was the burial site
I could excavate his body from. Temporary escapes are of no use,
you are playing house with a dismantling body.

(6) Do things that you enjoy.

Watch stand-up comedy on loop, Dave Chapelle, Chris Rock, Kevin Hart.
Get used to laughing at how crazy a betrayed woman is,
a man's favourite joke to tell.

(7) Pamper yourself.

I gave birth to a new version of me, learning love again like walking.

(8) Prepare for things that may trigger your grief.

Use the mute button — pretend you chose to make them a ghost.
Of all triggers, my reflection is the most consistent.
I am reminded I should be over this by now.

Removed from the Edge

After 'Edge' by Sylvia Plath. A remixed golden shovel.

The woman is perfected through the rewriting of the script,
        and in this version
her dead

body crawls back out of the oven,
in this ending her lungs are not a bruised parachute.
The illusion of a face flaunting a forged smile for years

flows out from its tired veil,
        carbon monoxide spits itself out of her veins.
Her bare

feet stand to exit the surrendering position.
We have come too far to put an end to our search for sanity.

Each loose rope posing as an alternative method of dying
        coils itself back into the cupboard.
One at a time, the angels welcome her back into her body.

Pitcher of worth, they sing falsettos to Sylvia.
She folds the suicide letters and throws

them back into the bin. Someday they might be recycled
        into the paper holder
of a rose; redemption comes in many forms. Sing with me, no bone

stiffens at the sound of breath any longer, let a sweet song spill
from the splintered mouth of a once-forgotten trumpet.

She is used to this routine, but today
her black hair has no trace of ash, today she hugs herself
        so tight her breath glues back into place.

Balloons

My father and I have not spoken about the time
a gun got closer to his skin than I have.
The shot sounded like a balloon had burst
but something thicker than air had escaped.

It was the time thieves stormed in with masks and guns.
It was the time we lived in that small flat in Mushin, Lagos.
Our purses were weightless as a slice of confetti, yet
hope was the gas we filled the balloons tied to our hands with.

The trigger never punctured my father's body,
but his voice was already a deflating thing.
The older I get I outgrow
          my desire for balloons.

My father is a brown balloon,
but unlike the ones at parties
I do not run to catch him
when he floats from me.

Judas

My father is reducing the radius of his friendship circle
    to make it easier for him to spot death's reflection.

        The little he knows from the Bible is Judas
    was able to kiss death unto Jesus because they were close.

In this town, neighbours pray before shaking hands.
    The rumour is that someone blended death into a soup

        and fed it to my grandfather
    and [abracadabra] he transformed into corpse.

My father dines alone, places mirrors on the other chairs.
    Paranoia is the arrow that has stabbed his Adam's apple.

        He once asked if tomato stew was blood.
    He strokes the stringy hairs on his eaten mango with pity.

In a voice deep as a black hole, my father
    tells me it is wise to be selective of your companion.

        Half of my father's friends are dead,
    a small circle of friends is not his choice.

Today, the doctor told my father he will need further tests
    to determine if cancer has kissed death unto his kidney,

        There is no one to blame but his body,
cancer is not a close friend, he cannot call this betrayal.

Closer

home

My father hugs me for the first time
in twenty-three years
and he feels like a house without walls.

fill out this questionnaire

1.) Is that a birthmark on your face?

2.) Do you still want to be an accountant?

3.) What is your favourite food?

4.) Why don't you call me more?

5.) Was your mother a better father?

6.) If I die will you cry?

medical report

I found the medical report. The thin white paper peeked out of the bookshelf like a white flag practising the position of surrender. Doctor claims his kidney might be hardening into a rock that can weigh his body into a casket. I slap on denial like a plaster. My father has dodged death many times, I do not ask if he will be fine. I assume so.

fear

The TV is on loud, tuned to WWE. He sits with his face resting on his palm. His fingers tremble as he presses the area around his kidney. The body is a remote control. You never know which organ is the button that will lead to a sad channel.

behind closed doors

I am still a tender child. Time heals slower than a plastic bag degrades. My body shrinks like a cloth washed in the wrong temperature. Still I pray for my father so much my palms are warm enough to burn my face.

the last supper

I break bread with my father and watch him chew to remind myself he had a mouth all this while. He babbles banter and my mouth plays the laughing track I recorded in preparation for this day. Last night he asked what I wanted to eat for dinner, served me a plate of forgiveness.

what we had in common

Today my father stood under the living room lightbulb,
the light drew features onto his face.

We point out our similar features, how my eyes also arch at the tip.
The more time we spend together, the more I realise
even our ghosts share DNA.

He has one hand pressed on the area where his kidney is,
I do not ask why, I pretend he is hungry
and I ask what he wants for dinner.

A Shattered Ghazal On Understanding Existence

Grief has no ex//piry age, my grandfather lived a full life
yet at the funeral my mother's eyes were like doors flung open by a flood.

Ex//plain why the pain of loss competes to outweigh the peace
the gone now ex//hale in.

I yawn rage in the basement of my mouth, tired of sending God
mixed signals on whether the wish is to live forever or not at all.

Ex//istence is a difficult song, a chorus of razor blades,
try learning the lyrics without becoming a carving of wounds.

Aren't we tired of the routine of ex//posing our questions
to microscopes that only spit back more questions?

Oh Theresa, we ex//ploit the death of others
to campaign the fear of our body being ex//ported back to its manufacturer.

For now, the body will continue to retire
and translate into an ex//plicit language.

and grab verses about eternal life
like she is grabbing a rope to es//cape the burning building of her mind.

Praise the routine of ex//tracting peace from memories.
My mother puts on a Johnny Nash song, zips open her father's name to check

the Tom Tom sweets he always brought home from work to cheer her up
have not ex//pired their bliss aftertaste, a crown of ants thirsting for them.

The child in you is still afraid of the dark, now you weep in a different pitch.
My mother sees her father's casket and shrinks. Grief has no ex//piry age.

Dead Man Walking

To be diagnosed
with what has no cure
is to be pronounced dead
while you are alive.
My grandfather's funeral
lasted four years,
the doctor tried
to slow down the shovel
pouring sand into his mouth.
Organs are pessimists,
they begin to shut down
once they hear rumours
you are dying,
they eavesdrop on the doctor
telling you what you have is incurable.
My grandfather's heart
was the last organ to give up.
Typical, the heart
strung along a dead thing
before deciding to let go.

Tailoring Grief

The tailor says you have to get measured
to make sure grief fits right on your body.
If grief fits too tight it will suck movement out of you,
make you as still as the dead you are mourning.
I once wore grief so tight on my body my ribs tangled into a bow.
The tailor also says wearing an oversized grief will turn you
into a tripping hazard. There is only so much a body can take,
even a plane has weight limits.
We lined up at the tailors to get measured
for my grandfather's funeral. The women for their Aso-oke,
the men for their Agbada. The orange material draped on the table.
It is our culture to celebrate in colour coordination.
I handed the tailor a torn page from *Genevieve* magazine
and pointed out the style I wanted.
Imagine if Mary wore a Gele for the funeral of Jesus,
tied it so tight she was dizzy
enough to feel absent from her body.
I picked up my cloth from the tailor on the seventh day.
The off-shoulder dress exposed my neck
so my dented collarbones could collect my tears.
At the funeral my grandmother wore a dress
with sleeves puffed like swollen lungs.
I held her, the tassels at the end of my dress dangled
like a rain of breathing tubes.
From afar our orange dresses looked like saliva dripping
from the gaping mouth of the sun.
The whole village watched in holy envy:
envy is only effective from afar, does not see the layers
of blood-stained threads that sew this body together.
Give me a culture that requires grief to be sewn
delicately on the body, I'll take it any day.

Reporting Live from Grandpa's Funeral

LOLA, REPORTER: Afternoon, 'Aye Nreti Eleya' by Sunny Ade is playing as the mourners proceed to the cemetery. The pall-bearers dance with the casket as it rests on their shoulders like a radio player. In our culture, it is believed dying at old age is the finest cloth God can wrap your breath in. Explains why I haven't observed any tears, but if you look closely at the faces of the mourners you'll see that my grandfather's casket is a dancing bullet, puncturing holes in the body of every family member.

At the front of the line are my father and his brothers. There are reports that their hands were once woven together like cobwebs on the roof of a dirty house; however, occasions like this remould you into newness.

(COMMERCIAL BREAK)

My grandpa has now been buried. The weather is currently 35°C. The canopies have been set up for the after-celebration, they stand like an umbrella of clouds lining this heaven we are replicating on earth.

Let me get a quick word from my grandma, who is sitting over at the high table.

(Lola bends both knees to traditionally greet her)

LOLA: How are you feeling Ma?

GRANDMA, WIFE OF DECEASED: Fine, go and help your mother serve food to the guests.

LOLA: Alright Ma.

She has not said much today, she has not eaten either.
This grief is the texture of a deflated airbag and can take
years to chew and digest.

Briefly, if you look four tables down, Aunty Morayo is selling
bags and fabrics to guests; survival takes no days off even
when the sky is an absent customer.

I'll keep you updated. From the looks of things, even when
joy is amputated, we are a village of hands acting as each
other's crutches.

The Vow

My grandmother lifted her veil at the funeral,
      through it the sun looked like a ripped patch
      of my grandfather's earthy brown skin.

The words *Till Death Do Us Part*
      are brushed over as lightly as baby hairs.

My grandmother brushed
      her shaking fingers over her thinning hairs,

stood at the altar of his casket
      and read a eulogy like a wedding vow
      to marry off her desire to live.

Both still wearing their wedding rings —
      real gold does not rust
      but the body does.

Her face as tense as an unripe fruit;
      grief can squeeze tears from even the stiffest things.

I almost dare to ask if *Till Death Do Us Part*
      means she will have to peel off her love for him
      at the same rate his skin will yawn off his bones.

Pass the Parcel

At my grandfather's funeral we pass around a dead man's name like a pass-the-parcel game, each person unwrapping a new layer of him. Grandma says he travelled the world, came back with a new pronunciation for a foreign food folded in his suitcase like a smuggled sin. Teasing but refusing the effacement of our accent was a form of bonding. My mother says when he wasn't working at the computer firm he was either listening to Jimmy Cliffe or Johnny Nash, laidback as a reggae beat, but with work hours stretching longer he became an offbeat shadow struggling to memorise the details of his children's lives. We scrape off the shimmering silk bow wrapped around his name and examine new layers. Aunty Carla says he had OCD, would send her back to re-iron his shirt if there were no crisp lines to testify of the pressed heat. I added how his gnarled hands glowed like the bark of a thick tree, how he would soak a seed into the soil and promise that the cure of something will grow. His Aloe Vera plants gave a new shine to my tumbleweed textured hair strands. When I see a flock of birds flying I know they are on their way to scratch a layer of the sky to get a peek of my grandfather in heaven. We peel and peel and find nothing more to uncover, nothing to wet the tongue, edges neat even in roughness. How can a man leave with no secrets? I heard after a man dies all his demons resurrect. This must be an exception. My mother gets up and mimics his dance to Johnny Nash's 'I Can See Clearly Now'. When we pass around his name, we hold it delicate as an egg, unsure of what we could find if we continue to crack it, afraid that peace is the fragile object inside it.

<h>Cutting Back on Work Shifts </h1>

<body>
<p> On earth we are small-scale gods
with Google as the manufactured Garden of Eden,
anything unknown is an apple we chew aggressively.
I watch you search <b> cure for Alzheimer's </b>,
you have scraped the mouse so many times
<img src=your fingers are rusted copper wires.jpg">
This ache has an ungodly texture. <p>

<p> Granddaughter, I wish I could have helped improve
the search engine results for a cure for this disease,
but all those years I worked as a computer engineer
my skill was in building a furnace for the fire,
I had no experience in extinguishing it. <p>

<p> Here in heaven, my once weighted body floats
<img src=the floors of heaven are cobbled with the gold
teeth of our wisest uncles we dismissed as eccentric.jpg"
width="infinite" height="infinite">
Prayers flood in like the email inbox of a busy office.
I will tell you more as I discover.

I still ponder on earth's curiosity,
how we press our bodies into megabytes of bricks
to build a Tower of Babel just to peek into heaven.
I have seen many **HTTP Error 404** messages
in my lifetime. I am the homepage of question marks.

I beg you, let the computer rest for a minute, exhale,
today let silence be your search engine for peace.
<body>

Moving on is Involuntary

The morning after | water from the bathroom tap falls
like slices of a broken window | Do not fear, a time will come
your body will wash off grief | without feeling its sharp kiss

In the park flowers bloom | others bend like melted screws
like they always did | but you notice it more
now you are sensitive | to dead things

You see boisterous children playing on the streets | you resist
the temptation | of telling them
the ground will someday scrape the body | into ash

The 10 p.m. news is still | in a relationship with grief
The Bible is still a textbook | you struggle to study some nights
the words feel like wool | other nights like pebbles stoning you

You look out | of the window
the once concrete sky | has already ironed black into silk
even the world has rehearsed | the routine of mourning

Death: Definitions (II)

/dɛθ/

noun

When your lungs feel like two dangling pages
of a torn-open Bible.

Or

The period when your body feels torn, thin as paper,
is a chance to read the scriptures
scribbled inside you as you glue each page back together.

Lazarus

As the mothers of dead sons watched Lazarus
come back to life, their spines collapsed
like a string unhooked from the moon,
joy struggled to filter through their bitter tongues.

A woman said "Lord, my son's buried body makes him
a lantern trapped in a black hole, he was an almost Doctor,
yet you crowned Lazarus as worthy to be returned,
a man whose name till now was a bouquet of shadows".

Another woman said "My son left behind a small child,
has his resurrection been an unanswered prayer
because God wants to be the only one bearing
father?"

The weeping women wanted to run back home, but
jealousy converts the eyes into surveillance cameras
monitoring the downfall of someone to dance about.
The weeping women waited to help Mary and Martha

cook dinner for the guests welcoming Lazarus back.
They smiled at Lazarus, served him food
like he was their son, washed his feet
like he was their son, Lazarus hugged them

tight as a newborn's grip on a finger. His sight too hazy
to see their hands were shields infested with termites.
Lazarus's bandages were coiled beside him like a serpent,
those with untreated wounds heard it hiss at them.

At night, the women held pictures of their dead sons,
wept, dreamt of strangling Lazarus
with the bandages he was unravelled from,
his body swinging from the cross they once prayed to.

Blessed Are the Mothers of a Dead Child

Blessed are the mothers of a dead child
for they manage to recover
after eating the fruit that grows
from planting your child's casket in the ground.

Blessed are the mothers of a dead child
They leave the clothes untouched and locked away
as if begging the dead child to outgrow the denial.
Each year goes past and the dead do not age,
the clouds are fragments
of icing from their untouched birthday cakes.

Blessed are the mothers of a dead child
No doctor can heal this kind of pain,
my grandmother became her own patient,
has taken two tablets of prayer every 4 hours for the past 60 years.

Blessed are the mothers of a dead child
were the words I said after
I learned of the uncle that never grew to reach my age.
How, at age 7, measles turned his lungs into faulty wings.
My grandmother's spirit stayed in limbo for years,
a curtain hanging from a broken hook.

Blessed are the mothers of a dead child
My grandmother tries to celebrate the brief beauty of his breath.
She says what use is sweeping grief under the carpet
when you can blend it to find the drop of sanity that will flow from it.

We Rebuke This Bad Death

Dami is dead.
A rope was found clinging to his neck.
We think it was a halo failed by gravity.

Is he from our tribe?
Our language has no translation for 'suicide'.
Someone in the village must have orchestrated voodoo.

Should we drench our bodies with anointing oil
so when the spirit of death tries to enter
it will drown like Egyptians in the Red Sea?

During interrogation, his wife swears her hands are clean,
claims he had been having money issues.
She uses the word 'depression' and our breaths sink.

The Yoruba proverb goes 'A kì í sunkún a-nìkàn-para-ẹ' —
a man who leaves his children to inherit disgrace
does not deserve weeping.

Should he have waited till old age to die a good death?
His mother named him Oluwadamisi; God spares me.
How could he rebuke his own name?

A mother does not bury a child she raised
without feeling like she is disturbing the ground
with her failure.

Who is paying for the funeral?
Should we bury him with the rope around his neck
and hope it turns into a halo?

Swimming

After my grandfather's funeral I stay away
from anywhere that sits below ground level.

At the beach I used to stand close enough
for the water to paint the walls of my scar-stained legs,

now I dangle by the shore, so stiff
children mistake me for a stale sandcastle.

My sister tells me I am boring for building borders,
but even Brighton beach now feels like a palette of dull colours.

I can't see someone swimming without thinking
about how a body of water can double as a graveyard.

Staying Alive

The hands of voodoo priests are sore
from mixing healing powders for a crowd of men

who fear God is as invisible
as the space between the grains of powders.

At church, the pastor sways a handkerchief,
says it is soaked with God's holy healing power,

and a sea of bodies, half-believers, half-desperate,
run to the altar with their sick loved ones.

Somewhere a doctor is being trained to prevent the word *dead*
wobbling on his tongue like a fallen star.

I am sat in a room bloated with family members,
sadness hangs in the air like our family portrait.

Our hands are retired from praying
and fasting for the healing of my grandfather,

his organs a language
now difficult to translate by the doctor.

Alive is a word so fragile,
even a baby's teeth can crack it open.

Where is Ja Rule to Make Sense of the Apocalypse

"Where is Ja Rule to make sense of all this" – Dave Chappelle

These days buildings bruise like bodies
and bodies break like brittle branches.
The world has threatened to end so many times,
I have become indifferent to destruction.
The Bible on my mother's bedside table pinches my arm,
begs me to be prepared for rapture,
claims heaven's gate has strict bouncers.

By the next morning I am immersed
in a WhatsApp group chat with Stacey and Stella
about hashtags and hash outs; we debate
which song transports our body to the womb of another world.

On the day the earth decides to become sand again
and shovels begin growing in place of trees
I want my small world to remain intact,
I want to practise denial without disturbance,
is that too much to ask?
I know every beginning has to have an ending,
I watched the end of my grandfather who was once a child,
was once a beginning.

Each time news of an apocalypse resurfaces
I want recycled statements from celebrities,
calling it absurd, sending their *thoughts*
and prayers to the shaken, offering their empty mansions
as hideouts, as handmade heavens.
How I wish like them I can pretend I am not a part of this,
but my ego is not a strong enough lamppost to tie my body to
and stop a fire from sweeping me off my bones.

I close my Bible after another attempt at understanding –
in all this I wonder where is Ja Rule
to make sense of the apocalypse?
Men like him seem to have been alive for infinity,
he was the soundtrack to our after-school parties
when I was small, before I knew the word apocalypse
or could contain its barb-wired syllables in my mouth.
I have never seen fear leak from his mouth.
He released an album in 2012
as if unbothered the world was predicted to end that year.

I need Ja Rule to scratch out my anxiety with his raspy voice
by adlibbing over the angels
when they pull out their trumpets on the last day.

Today I will pull the speakers closer, drown into music
and ignore the world cradling in the arms of a clock.
I play the albums *Pain in Love* and *The Last Temptation*
and my body feels like a cassette tape
winding the tangled knot in my stomach back into childhood.
What is nostalgia if not a fire-proof chamber?

Ja Rule should have a joint concert
with Ashanti so I can be locked away
unable to hear the world collapsing like an expired star.
'Always on Time' plays and I won't peek at my watch,
I will sneak in a prayer between each song just in case
the stage collapses and I need to be remembered
by another God.

Death Definition (III)

/dɛθ/

noun

The colour of our shock
when the valuable item stolen from a famous person
is their breath.

      Or

Michael Jackson's death
made us realise we are all made of the same clay,
anyone can be moulded into a grave plaque.

Portrait of Jesus in a Blue Robe

Jesus stares at me through a painting
of him wearing a blue robe,

Jesus wept
when my grandfather's face turned blue
after swinging from Alzheimer's.
He promised that even in indignity there is a purpose
and used his bruised body on the cross as reference.

Jesus wept
when I began to treat him like the siren
of an off-duty police car, I chose silence over prayer,
my heart so hard even Lazarus would have traded
the resurrection of my dead faith over his dead body.

Jesus wept
when I stopped using the hem of his garment
to clothe my frail parts, instead I chose to use the sky
as a shield, forgetting the sky is made of netted fabric.

Jesus wept
as my mother spoke
of how God is more appreciated in Nigeria,
how the 24/7 electricity in England is confusing
their children by posing as God's eternal light.

Jesus wept
for at the time of the painting
blue was a more expensive colour than gold,
but times change
and we invent new ways to cheapen God.

Psalm 151

[1] I was born crying
at the first sight of the world,
begging my mother to push me back in,
because the darkness of the womb is
holier than all the light in the world.

[2] The chances of living untainted
are as small as
the chances of skin surviving
direct contact with the sun.

[3] O God have mercy on me
for what I have become.
An infinite well of excuses
for why I grew distant from light.

[4] I am a staggering disciple.
A Red Sea searching for Moses
to grant it a new face.

[5] Call me typical human
tripping on mistakes.

[6] God do not judge me for what I have become.
I signalled my fear of being conquered
by the things I was created to conquer.

[7] Ask my mother for evidence,
she'll tell you I cried at
the first sight of the world.

[8] I could see *evil* trolling in the air,
a cigarette lodged between its fingers.

[9] I fought it off with a strength
I prayed my fists into.

[10] From then I knew I was unprepared
for this world of fighting darkness.

Notes

'The Unedited Version of The Lord's Prayer' takes its structure from the 'Lord's Prayer' from the Bible in Matthew 6 vs 9-13.

The steps in 'wikiHow To Find Things You Have Lost' are taken from the wikiHow guide 'How to Find Things You Lost'.

'Removed from the Edge': the first two words of each line are the first two words from the lines of the poem 'Edge' by Sylvia Plath.

Acknowledgements and Thanks

Many thanks to my family, editors, mentors and friends who have been a part of this process.

The poems 'Equilibrium', 'Judas', 'The Pastor's Daughter Refuses to Be a Circle' and 'Black Marilyn' were included in the portfolio that jointly won the 2018 Brunel International African Poetry Prize.

'Psalm 151' first appeared in the Barbican Young Poets anthology, *Impossible Things About Optimism* (2016).

Thank you to Jane Commane for believing in this collection. Thank you to Nathalie Teitler for your overwhelming support. Thank you to the teachers I have learned from: Jacob Sam-La Rose, Nick Makoha, Rachel Long, Bernardine Evaristo, Pascale Petit, Mimi Khalvati. To friends whose poems kept me writing too: Victoria Adukwei Bulley, Caleb Femi, Jolade Olusanya, Emmanuel Sugo. Thanks to Octavia Poetry Collective for being a safe space I needed.

Thank you to R. A. Villanueva for your advice and working with me through the early stages of writing the poems in this collection.

Thank you to my supportive mother, my vibrant sister, and my brother who is a fountain of light and the most honest editor.